Béla Bartók

Ten Hungarian Songs

for voice and piano

(1906)

Bartók Records & Publications

2002

This work was first performed in Budapest
on the eighth of October, 1968
by Terézia Csajbók, soprano
and Lóránt Szűcs, piano

The work was recorded by the same artists
on Hungaroton: SLPX 12114

International Standard Music Number: M-9012001-3-5

Four of the songs in this volume: 4. "*Ha bemegyek a csárdába . . .*", 6. "*Megittam a piros bort . . .*", 7. "*Ez a kislány gyöngyöt füz . . .*", 8. "*Sej, mikor engem katonának visznek . . .*" have been published previously in a volume titled *Az ifjú Bartók I, válogatott dalok, Der Junge Bartók I, ausgewählte Lieder* (The Young Bartók I, Selected Songs), bearing the information "© Copyright 1963 by Editio Musica, Budapest". They are reproduced herein with the kind permission of Editio Musica, Budapest.

Published by Bartók Records, P. O. Box 399, Homosassa, Florida 34487, U. S. A.

Bartók Records No. 705

Preface

Soon after having started collecting folk song, Béla Bartók and Zoltán Kodály prepared for publication a volume of songs with piano accompaniment, ten contributed by each composer, titled: *Magyar Népdalok* (Hungarian Folk Songs). The volume contained a preface signed by both composers, almost entirely suitable also to the present volume:

"There are two ways to present folk music for publication, depending on two different objectives. One is to bring together every song that originated in one population, keeping in mind the presentation of a complete picture regardless of the relative values of the individual songs; this might be something like 'a standard dictionary of folk songs'. It would be best to organize the material in the manner of a dictionary, as was done in the Finnish folk song collection edited by Ilmari Krohn (*Suomen Kansan Sävelmiä*, four sections as of 1906). The songs are presented carefully and faithfully in all their variations. Only such a collection can become the basis of any studies pertaining to folk songs.

"The other objective is to get the general public to know and appreciate folk songs. For this purpose the 'standard dictionary' is not satisfactory, since it contains weak and excellent material interspersed. Selections must be made from the best and presented in transcriptions not too foreign to the public's taste. The songs need new clothes once we bring them from the fields into the cities. But in urban dress they feel awkward, cramped. Their apparel must be so tailored as not to smother them. Whether the transcription be for chorus or piano, the accompaniment should attempt merely to make up for the lost fields and villages. In faithfulness, on the other hand, the popular edition should not be inferior to the complete one.

"Naturally the first kind of edition is possible only after the collecting of all the material has been completed. In our country, where this work just began, we cannot think of it for a considerable time. It is possible, however, to begin selecting the best material from that already collected. This publication was prepared from such selected songs for the general public; it serves, also, the first objective since all profits derived will be used for furthering the work of collecting.

"Some of the twenty songs are taken from the recordings of Béla Vikár, an industrious worker in Hungarian folklore for many years — we here thank him for his kind permission to utilize the songs; the rest are from recently inaugurated collections. Because of the conditions under which these will be performed in the home, the melodies appear in the accompaniment also. We shall not always adhere to this practice in later publications. (The success of the collecting work will determine when these may appear.) After all, we are making available material to be sung, not only to be played on the piano.

"We hope that these often primordial expressions of our culture would find at least half the love they deserve. It will take a long time for them to reach their due place in our musical life both with the public and in the home. A large portion of Hungarian society is not yet Hungarian enough, no longer sufficiently ingenious nor truly cultured enough to enable these songs to gain closer access to its heart. The Hungarian folk song in the concert hall! How strange this may sound now. That it should be mentioned in the same breath with the masterworks of world literature and with the — foreign folk song. But the time for this will inevitably arrive, when the music making of the Hungarian family will be dissatisfied with the lowest of foreign 'popular songs' and the products of the domestic 'folk song factories'. When there will be a truly Hungarian singer. When others, besides those few who pursue the exotic, will know there is a different kind of Hungarian folk song than '*Ritka búza*' and the '*Ityóka-pityóka*'.

"*Béla Bartók*
Zoltán Kodály

"Budapest
December, 1906"

This volume, known in Western editions as **Twenty Hungarian Folk Songs**, of 1906, by Bartók and Kodály (not to be confused with **Twenty Hungarian Folk Songs**, published in

1929, by Bartók) was expected to be followed by others — as hinted in the above preface. Although both Bartók and Kodály later published other folk songs with piano accompaniment, a sequel to the first joint edition did not materialize. Bartók did write, in 1906, another series of ten songs with piano, but he never offered them to be published. The present volume contains these ten songs.

Why did these arrangements languish unpublished throughout the composer's life? Without first attempting an answer, the following facts are known:

1) At Christmas, 1906, the songs were ready; Bartók gave the manuscript to the lady who was later to become Mrs. Zoltán Kodály:

"Dedicated to Emma Gruber as a Christmas present by one of the authors.

Bratislava, on Christmas day, 1906."

(This manuscript is now in the Bartók Archívum, Budapest.)

2) Three of the songs (Nos. 4, 6, 9) were subsequently determined not to be folk songs.

3) The composer published two of the songs — with different accompaniment — in subsequent publications: No. 2 (*Erdők, völgyek. . .*) in the 1929 **Twenty Hungarian Folk Songs**, as Vol. 1, No. 3; No. 3 (*Olvad a hó . . .*) in the **Eight Hungarian Folk Songs**, written during 1907-1917 and published in 1922, where it is the last item. No. 5 (*Fehér László . . .*) and No. 10 (*Kis kece lányom . . .*) became pieces for solo piano in the series **For Children**, Vol. 1, Nos. 25 and 17 respectively **(1943 revised edition)**. No. 1 (*Tiszán innen . . .*) was incorporated by Kodály into his operetta Háry János, written in 1925-7.

4) When the first series of songs, published in 1906, came to be reprinted, Bartók revised the work, deleting the fifth song and re-numbering No. 4/a and /b as Nos. 4 and 5. It is believed that he realized, after the 1906 version was already printed, that song No. 5 (*Ucca, ucca, ég az ucca. . .*) was not a genuine folk-song but an art song in folk style. Similarly, the series **For Children** (piano pieces based on folk songs) could be reprinted in the early 1940's and he made use of this opportunity to remove several items whose bases were, as was found later, art songs in folk style, leaving the revised edition with fewer numbers.

Thus, there are probably more reasons than one why Bartók never returned to these ten songs as first written. One reason probably was the less than enthusiastic reception of the first volume on the part of the public: it took 32 years for the first printed edition to be sold. However, there was market for such songs, as demonstrated by the later publication of folk songs with piano accompaniment written separately by both Bartók and Kodály.

As of 1906 Bartók was newly acquainted with the folk music heritage of the Hungarian people. In his autobiography (1921) he reported having started studying Hungary's folk music some time after 1902; at first his attention was directed to "what was then regarded as Hungarian folk music". By 1905 he realized that the Hungarian songs, regarded erroneously as folk songs, are "actually more or less trivial art songs in folk style", and he "began searching for the Hungarian peasant music then virtually unknown". In the first year of this research Bartók could not have yet fully developed the formula for recognition of the genuine article. After years of having studied folk music, he was able to determine which songs were inadvertently included in previous compositions labeled as "folk songs", or derived from folk melodies, and he removed from circulation such items when he had an opportunity. It is not surprising that Béla Bartók, an uncompromising man, could not suggest or authorize the publication of a volume labeled <u>folk songs</u> if he already knew that several items in it were <u>not</u> folk songs.

As time passed, five folk songs from the ten songs were brought before the public in different context, different attire or treatment, or by a different composer. This leaves only two folk songs among the ten that remained unpublished in any form during the composer's life and perhaps they simply did not find a home in a song cycle. Thus, the cycle as originally composed remained unpublished.

The next question then is: why are these published now?

Notwithstanding the above considerations, these songs with piano accompaniment were originally composed as one cycle. Although some of them saw daylight elsewhere, the original artistic treatment was not retained in the other publications. Through these songs we can witness Béla Bartók's handling of the accompaniment, the harmonic treatment: his contribution. The objective now is not the introduction of folk songs, decorated so as to be presentable to the city people, but to present Béla Bartók's treatment of the musical themes they provide — folk, or otherwise.

Bartók gave us an argument, in his article containing a rebuttal to some critics of composers incorporating folk melodies into their works:

"The question is not simple. It is a grave mistake to attribute excessive significance to the subject, the theme, and that is an incorrect point of view. Don't these people realize that Shakespeare, for instance, never even wrote a work whose story, theme, he invented himself. Is it because Shakespeare's brain was so desiccated that he had to knock on door after door begging for handouts of themes for his works? Did Shakespeare try to cover up his inner lack of inventive talent? The case of Molière is even more conspicuous. He took over not only themes, but also details of construction of original texts, even copied expressions and whole lines. We know that one of Handel's oratories is nothing more than the remodeling of a work by Stradella. The remodeling is so masterful, so much above the level of the original, that it does not even remind us of Stradella. Can we speak here of plagiary, of a dried out talent? No more than of Shakespeare when he took over a Marlow tragedy, or of Molière when he dipped into a Spanish source, or of Stravinsky when he made use of folk themes, or themes of other foreign origin, in many of his works.

"What in a literary work is the story, corresponds in music to the thematic material. But in musical art, just as in literature, sculpture or painting, what is important is not the choice of theme we make use of, but what we do wih it. The artist's competence, his power of creative expression, his individuality, becomes revealed in this 'what'."

With these considerations Béla Bartók's ten Hungarian songs are brought before the public. In this album we find songs of mixed origin — genuine folk, art in popular style — treated with harmonies and accompaniment by a 25 year young musician who was destined to become one of the foremost composers of the century.

*   *   *

Notes

Although the cycle of songs published in 1906 and those in this volume were composed in the same year, the musical treatment in the two cases differs. In the first series the piano accompaniment includes the melody — as noted in the authors' preface to that volume — to help singers not yet at home in the style of the old Hungarian folk songs. In accordance with the prediction in the preface ("in future publications we may not adhere to this pattern"), we no longer find the melody in the piano part of the present volume, allowing the accompanying voice to roam freely within its own territory.

In the 1906 song cycle tempi are only verbally indicated, e.g. "dance-steps", "slowly", "very slowly", etc. The explanation is in the Notes: ". . . we must not believe that every song must have its own tempo defined by law: the 'folk'-people often perform the very same song at widely different tempi. It is the performer's task to find the tempo that renders the song most effectively."

In the same fashion, dynamics are seldom directed for the vocal line. As explanation in the Notes: "The 'folk'-people do not recognize dynamics. Their singing is louder or softer on different occasions, but there is no variation [within a performance] other than the inherent changes that occur with rising or falling pitch. The artistic performance may not exist without dynamic coloring, but just in folk songs one must provide the minimum of guidance. Yet, we do not suggest that the only proper rendition of a folk song would be the strict imitation of its folk-performance. Then, for instance, say No. 11 [in the 1906 publication] would have to be stretched out and ornamented the way it is done by old women in church. Yet, it is not at all inconceivable that the true song artist should reveal to us elements of beauty in a folk song that remain hidden in its performance by the folk."

In the manuscript of the present volume dynamics and tempi are scarce; these are editorially supplied in print, but sparingly. Additions affecting pitch, tempo or dynamics are indicated by smaller size characters, brackets, or slash. As to additions of lesser significance, a facsimile of the manuscript is included at the end of this volume for reference.

Peter Bartók

1.

BÉLA BARTÓK
(1881-1945)

Ti- szán in- nen, Ti- szán túl,

Túl ____ a Du- nán van egy csi- kós ____ nyá - jas -

tul. ____

BR 705

2.

E- sik e-ső az e - gek - bül,

Ró - zsa nyí-lik az völ- gyek - bül. Hát én csak ma -

gam e - gye- dül Hogy él - jek meg ná - lad nél - kül?

3.

há - rom - e - me - le - tes ma - gos ka - szár - nyá - ba. Nem le - he - tek

én ró - zsa, el - her - vaszt Fe - renc Jós - ka, A nagy bé - csi

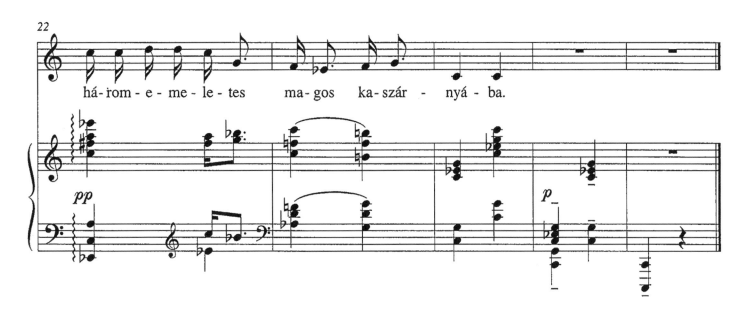

há - rom - e - me - le - tes ma - gos ka - szár - nyá - ba.

4.

Tánclépés [Moderato, tempo giusto]   *f (mf la 2ª volta)*
grazioso

1. Ha be - me - gyek a csár - dá - ba,
2. Ha be - me - gyek a csár - dá - ba,

pp

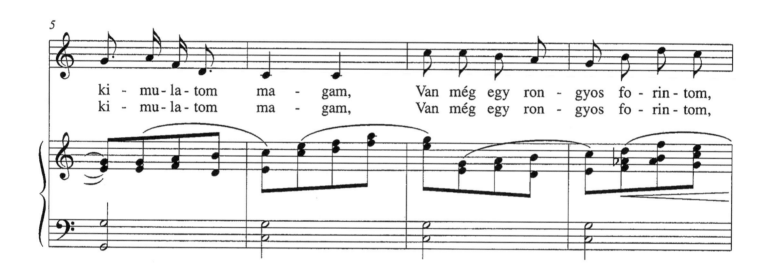

ki - mu - la - tom ma - gam, Van még egy ron - gyos fo - rin - tom,
ki - mu - la - tom ma - gam, Van még egy ron - gyos fo - rin - tom,

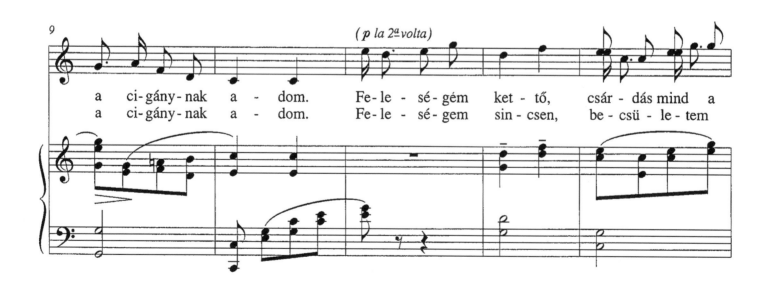

(p la 2ª volta)

a ci - gány - nak a - dom. Fe - le - sé - gém ket - tő, csár - dás mind a
a ci - gány - nak a - dom. Fe - le - sé - gem sin - csen, be - csü - le - tem

5.

6.

[Moderato, tempo giusto]

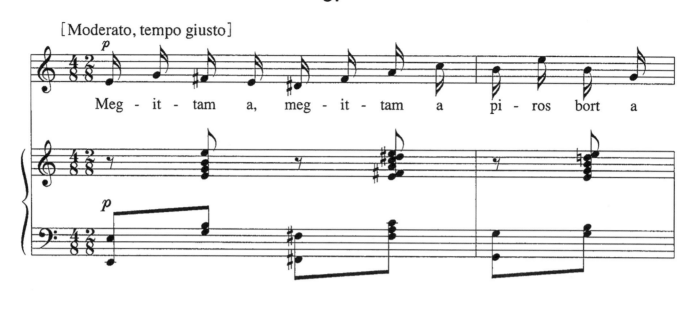

Meg - it - tam a, meg - it - tam a pi - ros bort a

po - hár - bul, Kár vol - na még ki - mul - nom a vi - lág - bul,

Kár vol - na még meg - hal - ni, I - lyen ko - rán hër - vad - ni,

A sze - le - i, kis sze - le - i te - me - tő - be hër - vad - ni.

Kár vol - na még meg - hal - ni, I - lyen ha - mar hër - vad - ni,

A sze - le - i, kis sze - le - i te - me - tő - be hër - vad - ni.

7.

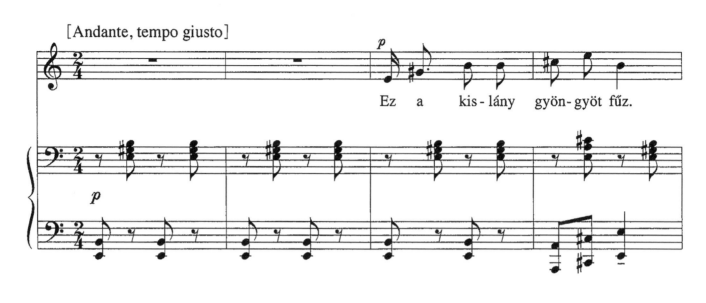

[Andante, tempo giusto]

Ez a kis-lány gyön-gyöt fűz.

Ég a sze-me mint a tűz, Ha jaz e-nyém úgy ég - ne,

Csu-ha-ha, bar-na le-gény sze-ret - ne. De mi - vel hogy nem úgy ég,

Csu-ha-ha, bar-na le-gény rám se néz.

A ha-rasz-ti ha-tá-ron Csősz le-szek én a nyá-ron.

A-ki né-kem csó-kot ád, Csu-ha-ha, nem haj-tom be a lo-vát;

Sem a lo-vát, sem ma-gát, Csu-ha-ha, sem a ked-ves ga-lamb-ját.

BR 705

8.

Sej, mi-kor ën - gem ka-to - ná - nak visz - nek,

Mind le-hull-nak a nyár - fa - le - ve - lek. Sír - hat - tok már,

be - ne - de-ki lá - nyok, Sej, há-rom é - vig nem já - rok hoz -

9.

[Andante]

Még azt mond-ják, sej, haj, i - ciny - pi - ciny az én ba-bám.
Ha tán - co-lok vé - le, nem is il - lik ő én-hoz-zám.

Tyu-haj, nem is bá - nom, a - kár - mi - lyén i-ciny-pi-ciny vagy,

Nagy az én sze - rel - mem, így is, úgy is az e-nyém vagy.

10.

Texts

There is no attempt to provide English words to be sung with these melodies; indeed, when this is done, the results are less than satisfactory once words of different rhythm are substituted for the text the melodies originally evolved with. The following translations are intended merely to convey the subject matter, the mood, of the songs. Repeats of lines or sections are not shown.

1.
Tiszán innen, Tiszán túl,
Túl a Dunán van egy csikós nyájastul.
Kis pej lova ki van kötvel,
Szürkötéllel, pakróc nélkül, gazdástul.

On this side of the Tisza, beyond the Tisza,
Beyond the Tisza lives a horseman with his herd.
His little bay horse is tied up,
With a felt rope, without a rug, with his master.

Tiszán innen, Tiszán túl,
Túl a Dunán van egy gulás nyájastul.
Legelteti a guláját,
Oda várja a babáját gyep ágyra.

On this side of the Tisza, beyond the Tisza,
Beyond the Danube there is a herdsman with his flock.
He lets his flock graze,
He awaits his sweetheart with a bed of sward.

2.
Erdök, völgyek, szük ligetek,
Sokat bujdostam bennetek;
Bujdostam én az vadakkal,
Sírtam a kis madarakkal.

Forests, valleys, tight groves,
For a long time I was hiding among you;
I was a fugitive with the wild game,
I wept with the little birds.

Esik esö az egekbül,
Rózsa nyílik az völgyekbül.
Hát én csak magam egyedül
Hogy éljek meg nálad nélkül?

The rain is falling from the skies,
Roses bloom in the valleys.
I just continue all alone,
How can I live without you?

3.
Olvad a hó, csárdás kisangyalom,
    tavasz akar lenni.
De szeretnék kiskertedben
    rózsabimbó lenni!
Nem lehetek én rózsa,
    elhervaszt Ferenc Jóska,
A nagy bécsi háromemeletes
    magos kaszárnyába.

The snow is melting, my sweetheart,
    spring is on its way.
How I would like to be a rosebud
    in your garden!
But I can not be a rose,
    Francis Joseph is sure to wilt me,
In the big tall three storey
    barracks of Vienna.

4.
Ha bemegyek a csárdába,
    kimulatom magam,
Van még egy rongyos forintom,
    a cigánynak adom.
Feleségem kettö,
    csárdás mind a kettö,
Reméllem, hogy jövö összel
    reng a cifra böcsö.

When I go to the inn
    I have a good time.
I have one lousy florin left,
    I give it to the gypsy.
I have two wives,
    both are attractive,
I hope that by next autumn
    the painted cradle will be rocking.

Ha bemegyek a csárdába,
    kimulatom magam,
Van még egy rongyos forintom,
    a cigánynak adom.
Feleségem sincsen,
    becsületem sincsen,
Belenyúlok a zsebembe:
    egy krajcárom sincsen.

When I go to the inn
    I have a good time.
I have one lousy florin left,
    I give it to the gypsy.
I have no wife at all,
    neither have I honor,
I reach into my pocket:
    I find not a single farthing.

I

5.

Fehér László lovat lopott
    a fekete halom alatt.
Hej! Fehér Lászlót ott megfogták,
    tömlöc fenekére zárták.

6.

Megittam a piros bort a pohárbul
Kár volna még kimulnom a világbul.
Kár volna még meghalni,
Ilyen korán hërvadni,
A szelei, kis szelei temetöbe hërvadni.
Kár volna még meghalni,
Ilyen hamar hërvadni,
A szelei, kis szelei temetöbe hërvadni.

7.

Ez a kislány gyöngyöt füz,
Ég a szeme mint a tüz.
Ha jaz enyém úgy égne
Csuhaha, barna legény szeretne.
De mivelhogy nem úgy ég,
Csuhaha, barna legény rám se néz.

A haraszti határon
Csösz leszek én a nyáron.
Aki nekem csókot ád
Csuhaha, nem hajtom be a lovát;
Sem a lovát, sem magát,
Csuhaha, sem a kedves galambját.

8.

Sej, mikor ëngem katonának visznek
Mind lehullanak a nyárfalevelek.
Sírhattok már, benedeki lányok,
Sej, három évig nem járok hozzátok.

Sej, mikor ëngem katonának visznek
Az árokban még a víz is reszket.
Az árokban a víz hadd reszkessen,
Sej, csak a babám igazán szeressen.

9.

Még azt mondják, sej haj,
    iciny-piciny az én babám.
Ha táncolok véle,
    nem is illik ö énhozzám.
Tyuhaj, nem is bánom
    akármilyen iciny-piciny vagy,
Nagy az én szerelmem,
    így is, úgy is az enyém vagy.

10.

Kis kece lányom fehérbe vagyon,
Fehérbe rózsám, fehérbe vagyon.
Mondom, mondom, fordulj hozzám,
    mátkám asszony,
Mondom, mondom, fordulj hozzám,
    mátkám asszony.

László Fehér stole a horse
    under the black hills.
Hey! László Fehér got caught there,
    and thrown into the dungeon.

I drank the glass of red wine,
It would be sad to leave the world now.
It would be a pity to die now,
To wilt so early,
To wilt in the cemetery of Szele, Kisszele.
It would be a pity to die now,
To wilt so soon,
To wilt in the cemetery of Szele, Kisszele.

This little girl is threading pearls
Her eyes sparkle, like fire.
If mine sparkled the same way
Hey, ho, the brown haired lad would love me.
But as they do not sparkle so,
Hey, ho, he does not even notice me.

On the estate of Haraszt
I will serve as guard this summer.
If someone gives me a kiss
Hey-ho, I will not capture her horse,
Neither the horse, nor herself,
Not even her sweetheart.

Hey, when they take me into the army
All the poplar leaves will drop off.
Mourn me, girls of Benedek,
Hey, I will not visit you for three years.

Hey, when they take me into the army
Even the water in the ditch trembles.
Let the water tremble in the ditch,
Hey, as long as my sweetheart loves me truly.

People gossip, hey ho,
    my sweetheart is so tiny.
When I dance with her
    we do not match at all.
Heyahey, I could not care less
    how tiny you may be,
Great is my love for you,
    you are mine all the same.

My little girl is dressed in white,
My sweetheart is in white, dressed in white.
I say: turn towards me,
    my betrothed woman,
I say: turn towards me,
    my betrothed woman.

Song No. 5 (Fehér László . . .) is one of many variants about a notorious horse-thief. The variant used has only one stanza, presenting the essence of the story. Following is the text of a longer variant[1]:

Fehér László lovat lopott	László Fehér stole a horse
A fekete halom alatt,	Under yonder murky hills.
Hatot fogott suhogóra,	Six he caught
Görc városa csodájára.	And the city of Görc wondered at the deed.
Rajta, rajta Görc városa,	Arise, arise, city of Görc,
Fehér László meg van fogva.	László Fehér is caught.
Verjünk vasat a kutyára,	The cur will be put in irons,
Jobb kezére, bal lábára.	His right hand chained to his left foot.
"Kutya betyár, add meg magad,	"Dog of an outlaw, give yourself up,
Vagy azt mondd meg, kinek hínak.	Or tell us what is your name.
Kutya betyár, add meg magad,	Dog of an outlaw, give yourself up,
Vagy azt mondd meg, kinek hínak."	Or tell us what is your name."
"Az én lovam keselylábú,	"My horse has piebald legs,
Az én húgom Fehér Anna."	My young sister is Anna Fehér."
"Nem kérdjük mink a lovadat,	"We do not inquire about your horse,
Sem azt a büszke húgodat."	Nor about your proud sister."
"Kutya betyár, add meg magad,	"Dog of an outlaw, give yourself up,
Vagy azt mondd meg, kinek hínak.	Or tell us what is your name.
Kutya betyár, add meg magad,	Dog of an outlaw, give yourself up,
Vagy azt mondd meg, kinek hínak."	Or tell us what is your name."
"Az én lovam keselylábú,	"My horse has piebald legs,
Az én nevem Fehér László."	And my name is László Fehér."
"Verjünk vasat a kutyára,	"Let's put the fetters on the cur:
Jobb kezére, bal lábára."	Tie his right hand to his left foot."
El is vitték jó messzire,	And they led him far away,
Sötét börtön fenekére.	And they thrust him in a dark prison.
El is vitték jó messzire,	And they led him far away,
Sötét börtön fenekére.	And they thrust him in a dark prison.
Fehér Anna meghallotta,	Anna Fehér heard the news
Hogy a bátyja be van fogva.	That her brother was caught.
Parancsolja kocsisának:	So she told her coachman:
"Kocsisom, fogj be hat lovat,	"Coachman, harness up six horses,
Kocsisom, fogj be hat lovat,	Coachman, harness up six horses,
Tégy fel egy véka aranyat,	Load on a bushel of gold pieces,
Tégy fel egy véka aranyat,	Load on a bushel of gold pieces,
Kiszabadítom bátyámat."	For me to buy my brother's freedom."
Fehér Anna nem nyúgodott,	Anna Fehér did not tarry,
Felszaladt a vasajtóra:	She went to the iron door.
"Bátyám, bátyám, Fehér László,	"Brother, brother, László Fehér,
Aluszol-e, vagy nyúgodol?"	Are you asleep, or are you resting?"
"Se nem alszok, se nem nyugszok,	"I am neither asleep, nor resting,
Húgom, rólad gondolkozok.	Little sister, I think of you!
Se nem alszok, se nem nyugszok,	I am neither asleep, nor resting,
Húgom, rólad gondolkozok."	Little sister, I think of you!"

---

[1] Song No. 29 in **The Hungarian Folk Song**, by Béla Bartók, Bartók Records, Homosassa, FL, 2003.

III

Fehér Anna nem nyúgodott,
Felszaladt a vasajtóra:
"Bátyám, bátyám, Fehér László,
Hogy hívják itten a bírót?"

"Ez a bíró Horvát bíró,
Az akasztófára való.
Ez a bíró Horvát bíró,
Az akasztófára való."

Ekkor megyen Fehér Anna
Horvát bíró ablakára:
"Bíró, bíró, Horvát bíró,
Szabadítsd ki a bátyámat,

Szabadítsd ki a bátyámat,
Adok egy véka aranyat."
"Nem kell nékem az aranyad,
Csak hálj vélem egy éjcaka."

Fehér Anna nem nyúgodott,
Felszaladt a vasajtóra:
"Bátyám, bátyám, Fehér László,
Azt mondta nekem a bíró:

'Kiszabadul bátyád még ma,'
Háljak véle eggy éjcaka.
'Kiszabadul bátyád még ma,'
Háljak véle eggy éjcaka."

"Húgom, húgom, Fehér Anna,
Ne hálj véle egy éjcaka;
Szüzességedet elveszi,
A bátyádnak fejét veszi."

Fehér Anna nem nyúgodott,
Elment a bíró házához,
Véle is hált egy éjcaka
Az aranyos nyoszolyába.

Éjféltájban egy órakor
Csörgés esett az udvaron.
"Bíró, bíró, Horvát bíró,
Mi csörömpöl az udvaron?"

"Kocsisom lovát itatja,
Annak csörög zabolája.
Kocsisom lovát itatja,
Annak csörög zabolája."

Fehér Anna nem nyúgodott,
Felszaladt a vasajtóra:
"Bátyám, bátyám, Fehér László,
Aluszol-e, vagy nyúgodol?"

"Húgom, húgom, Fehér Anna,
Ne keresd itt a bátyádat:
Zöld erdöbe, zöld mezöbe,
Akasztófa tetejébe!"

Anna Fehér did not tarry,
She went to the iron door.
"Brother, brother, László Fehér,
Tell me who is judge here."

"The judge here is Judge Horvát,
A gallows-bird indeed,
The judge here is Judge Horvát,
A gallows-bird indeed!"

Thereupon went Anna Fehér
Under Judge Horvát's window.
"Hearken, Judge, Judge Horvát!
Set my brother free,

Set my brother free,
I shall give you a bushel of gold pieces."
"I do not want your bushel of gold pieces,
I only want a night with you!"

Anna Fehér did not tarry,
She went to the iron door.
"Brother, brother, László Fehér,
This the judge said to me:

'Your brother will be set free at once,'
But I must spend the night with him.
'Your brother will be set free at once,'
But I must spend the night with him."

"Sister, sister, Anna Fehér,
Do not spend the night with him.
He will rob you of your maidenhood,
And cut off your brother's head."

Anna Fehér did not tarry,
Went to the judge's house,
And she spent the night with him
In his golden bed.

And at the hour of midnight
A clatter arose from the courtyard.
"Hearken, Judge, Judge Horvát,
What is this clatter in the courtyard?"

"My coachman is watering my horse,
And so the bit is rattling.
My coachman is watering my horse,
And so the bit is rattling."

Anna Fehér did not tarry,
She went to the iron door.
"Brother, brother, László Fehér,
Are you asleep, or are you resting?"

"Sister, sister, Anna Fehér,
Do not seek your brother here,
But in the green woods, in the green fields,
Hanging from the gallows."

Akkor megyen Fehér Anna
Horvát bíró ablakára:
"Bíró, bíró, Horvát bíró,
Lovad lába megbotoljon,

Lovad lába megbotoljon,
Tégedet a földhöz vágjon.
Lovad lába megbotoljon,
Tégedet a földhöz vágjon.

Tizenhárom szekér szalma
Rothadjon el az ágyadban,
Tizenhárom esztendeig
Nyomjad az ágyad fenekit.

Tizenhárom doktor keze
Fáradjon ki sebeidbe,
Tizenhárom sor patika
Ürüljön ki a számodra.

Úgy-e bíró, jót kívánok:
Mosdóvized vérré váljon,
Törülköződ lángot hányjon,
Isten téged meg ne áldjon!"

Thereupon went Anna Fehér
Under Judge Horvát's window:
"Hearken, Judge, Judge Horvát,
May your horse stumble on his feet,

May your horse stumble on his feet,
And you be thrown to the ground.
May your horse stumble on his feet,
And you be thrown to the ground!

May thirteen cartloads of straw
Rot away in your bed!
May you for thirteen years
Lie upon it in cruel illness!

May thirteen doctors work
At dressing your wounds,
Thirteen shelves of drugs
Be emptied on your account!

Indeed, Judge, I wish you well:
May your washing-water turn to blood,
Your towel spit flames,
And God never bless you!"

* * *

Facsimile of the manuscript

4.

In the catalog of Bartók Records

All works by Béla Bartók unless otherwise noted

<u>Sheet music</u>

Cadenzas (Cca 1939)
    to Concerto for Two Pianos and Orchestra in E♭ major by W. A. Mozart, K.365
        Prepared for publication by Nelson O. Dellamaggiore,
        with an introduction by Ferenc Bónis   **BR700**

The Husband's Grief, for voice and piano (1945)   **BR701**

Fifteen Hungarian Peasant Songs
    corrected and edited by Peter Bartók   ***BR702**

Allegro Barbaro, for piano
    corrected and edited by Peter Bartók   ***BR703**

        * These items may not be sold in Great Britain or Europe

<u>Manuscript facsimiles</u>

Viola Concerto sketches (1945)
    includes also engraved fair copy prepared by Nelson O. Dellamaggiore
    with introduction by László Somfai   **BR800**

Liebeslieder (1900)
    with an introduction by Ferenc Bónis   **BR801**

<u>Books</u>

My Father, by Peter Bartók   **BR500**

Turkish Folk Music from Asia Minor
    revised according to the manuscript   **BR501**

The Hungarian Folk Song
    corrected edition   **BR502**

<u>Compact discs</u>

Bartók: **Dance Suite, Miraculous Mandarin Suite,** Bartók-Serly: **Mikrokosmos Suite**
    New Symphony Orchestra of London, Tibor Serly, Franco Autori   **BR1301**

Beethoven: **String Quartets, Opus 59, No. 3; Opus 14, No. 1**
    New Music String Quartet   **BR1909**

Liszt: **Variations on the Prelude:** *"Weinen, klagen, . . ."* by J. S. Bach; *Weihnachtsbaum,*
    excerpts; Bartók: **Three Rondos, Sonatina,** Excerpts from **For Children**
    Ilona Kabos, piano   **BR1910**

Bartók: **Two Sonatas for violin and piano**
    Robert Mann, Leonid Hambro   **BR1922**

<u>LP (vinyl) records</u> listed at **our website**

Bartók Records, P. O. Box 399, Homosassa, Florida 34487

www.bartokrecords.com